CREATING YOUR BUSINESS
VISION

a step-by-step guide for designing
the work you've always wanted to do

MICHAEL NICHOLS

Author of *One-on-One Meetings that Work*

Copyright © 2013 by Michael Nichols.
All rights reserved. No portion of this publication may be reproduced or transmitted in any form by any means – except for brief quotations in published reviews – without the prior written consent of the author.

ISBN-13: 978-1493623051

ISBN-10: 1493623052

Contents

Do You Know Where You Are Headed?	7
A Struggling Leader	9
One Important Rule	13
The Basics	15
Which Is It?	17
Vision Is What You Will Become	21
Let's Get Started!	23
Core Convictions	25
Core Purpose	29
Envisioned Future	33
Huge Goals	35
Vivid Description	39
Get It All Together	45
Review and Communicate It	47
A Growing Leader	49
Your Voice Matters	53
Resources	55
Building Champions	57
Contact	59
Share It With Others!	61

For Madison.
May you live, love, and lead
with vision and passion.

Do You Know Where You Are Headed?

Most organizations have a vision statement somewhere in a file or on a conference room wall. Yet, unfortunately, these vision statements rarely lead to exponential growth and remarkable success for the organization.

In a recent meeting with a university department team, I asked them how developing a Business Vision could help their team. Every member of the team believed that a department vision would significantly enhance collaboration, communication, and performance.

Several team members expressed that they had seen organizational vision statements but had never seen a vision for an individual, for a team, or for a department. And they had never considered developing one.

CREATING YOUR BUSINESS VISION

While creating a vision for your work can be one of the most challenging experiences in your life and career, it will be one of the most rewarding.

A vision is energizing. It's enlivening. Vision is the guiding motivation for all great human efforts.

Before we jump into vision, it's important to note that your Business Vision will be most useful if you understand how your life fits into your overall work. Developing a life plan is a great way to assess how your life and work complement each other. For help on this, I highly recommend Michael Hyatt's eBook, *Creating Your Personal Life Plan*.

While it's not imperative that you develop a life plan first, Michael's eBook is really the prequel to this book.

Your vision will have deeper meaning and greater clarity, when it is developed in conjunction with a healthy life plan.

A Struggling Leader

Early in my career, I experienced a number of incredibly difficult challenges in a relatively short period of time. I know you've been there too.

Although my team was experiencing record-setting achievements, relationships were strained and my influence was dwindling. I couldn't make sense of it. I didn't understand why my colleagues resented my passion for my work, my aggressive goals, and the long hours I put in.

I loved my work. I loved the outcomes. I loved my team. I loved how they were growing.

But it never occurred to me that my passion, energy, and achievements would intimidate those around me.

After all, I was laser-focused on improving the organization we were all part of.

Their fear morphed into resentment. I began pushing harder, defending the vision and strategy, and reacting to challenges.

As you might imagine, none of this improved the situation. In fact, it made matters worse. Finally, two administrators shared with me what should have been obvious —

"Michael, your team doesn't trust you. Some don't even like you."

This feedback was extremely painful for me to accept and even more difficult for me to understand and process. I was in denial. I simply could not bring myself to see from their perspective. Yet I was convinced that the work environment was not sustainable — for me or for my team.

So, on the recommendation of a friend, I hired Building Champions executive coach Raymond Gleason to help me work through life and business planning, priority management, and decision-making.

This decision was a life-changer for me. In fact, shortly after I made this decision, Sarah (my wife) and I sat at dinner with several of our friends while they joked about how differently I now approach my life and work.

My experience with creating a life plan and a Business Vision, regularly reviewing them, and updating them, has been transformational.

These documents have kept me on track as my family, friends, career, and other interests have grown.

My life and work are fast-moving. And when work gets hectic, my Business Vision and plans get me back on the path to my envisioned destination.

Creating your Business Vision can change how you approach your life and work forever.

Are you ready?

One Important Rule

Creating your Business Vision will take much thought and time. You will need to do some deep thinking, even some soul-searching to create something that is of value. So, I have **one important rule**...

Your vision should be completed in an environment that helps you to think deeply and creatively.

If you are working on a career vision or a vision for your position, I recommend that you **plan a minimum of a full day away to work on your vision**.

Get away from home, away from the office, away from distractions. Go on a retreat, visit a park, the mountains, the beach – go somewhere you will not be interrupted or distracted by your phone, email, or people.

Don't take your computer, tablet, or smart phone. Writing out your vision by hand is an important part of the process – it helps with reflection, processing, and deep thinking.

If you are working on a vision with your team, plan the day away from the office. Consider a local restaurant, clubhouse, or hotel meeting room that is quiet and free from distractions and where you'll have plenty of room to work. Take a white board, flip chart, and easel.

Have fun with it!

The Basics

I don't have to tell you that personal growth and organizational growth require clear, compelling vision. Developing a vision – **what your work will become** – and getting it down on paper will allow you to create very specific plans for accomplishing it.

So, where do we start? In this book, I will share with you step-by-step how to create a vision for your work. Your Business Vision will help you move forward with clear intent and purpose.

Your vision doesn't need to be long. My own vision is surprisingly short – less than two pages long. It consists of four sections:

Core Convictions
Core Purpose
Huge Goals
Vivid Description

Which Is It?

Before you get started, it is important to decide the type of Business Vision you are working on – **career vision, position vision, team vision, or organization vision**. While this tool will effectively guide you through each of these, the type of vision will determine your perspective, how you answer questions as you work through this guide, and how you craft your vision.

Throughout the book I will refer to "the organization" – if you are working on a career, team, or position vision, just substitute the term that describes the vision type you are working on.

So, let's figure out which one makes the most sense for you at this time...

Career Vision. If you're just starting out in your career or you are considering a career change, you are going to complete a vision for your career.

Position Vision. Have you been working in your field, organization, or position for a while? Are you planning to continue in this position or a similar position? A position vision is specific to your area of responsibility. Keep in mind that your position vision is always subject to the approval of your supervisor.

Team Vision. If you lead a team or you are part of a team that is working together to develop a vision, this tool can guide your team discussions and the development of a team vision. A team vision is a collaborative effort with your team. Check out the step-by-step guide for developing a team vision with your team at www.michaelnichols.org/developing-vision.

Organizational Vision. Do you lead an organization? Or are you launching a new company? If so, you will be developing an organizational vision. An organizational vision will greatly benefit from collaboration with key stakeholders.

If you do not lead the organization, it is important that you work on a vision for your area of responsibility. Developing a vision for an organization that you do not lead will only frustrate you, your team, and those you follow.

WHICH IS IT?

So, which is it? Write down the type of vision that you are going to create.

_____

_____

Remember, as you work through the rest of the book, to replace "organization" with the appropriate type of vision you're working on - career, position, or team vision.

Vision Is What You Will Become

And if you can see it, you can build it. (Daniel Harkavy, CEO, Building Champions)

So, what do you see?

Your answer to this question will help you to develop the vision and strategy to move forward with clear intent and purpose, whether you are leading a team of 100 or simply leading yourself.

When complete, your vision will act as a giant magnet pulling you forward, regardless of challenges and crises that occur.

Your vision begins with you addressing your **Core Convictions** and **Core Purpose** which answer the following questions: What are the indispensable beliefs that make you who you are? What do you stand for? Why do you exist?

CREATING YOUR BUSINESS VISION

Next, you will identify one or more **huge, long-term goals** and develop a **vivid description** of what the future of your business will look like.

Going through this process will provide a target to aim for as your business grows and changes. It will also allow you to communicate your vision to those around you.

Now, you are ready to craft your Business Vision.

You are about to create a vision that will serve as a constant guide for your life's work for years to come.

Let's Get Started!

We all want to belong to something – something bigger than ourselves.

Vision is the invitation to others to belong to something compelling, something bigger, something great.

So, ask yourself: What do I, or what does my team, want to belong to? Who are we?

You are trading your time to work with your team and organization. And people are trading their time to work together with you – **are they trading it for something that is worthwhile?**

Core Convictions

We start with Core Convictions – the driving passion in our heart; what motivates us. Here's how Daniel Harkavy, CEO of Building Champions, describes Core Convictions:

> Some call them core values. I like Core Convictions because convictions are stronger than values. And the term convictions clearly communicates that they are non- negotiable.
>
> Core Convictions are not the same as values – they are stronger than values. They define what we stand for. They are worth fighting for and taking significant risk for. They are non-negotiable. They are portable – we would take them with us no matter where we work.

Core Convictions must be authentic and discovered within the organization (or department or yourself, depending on the type of vision you are creating). They are intrinsic, not aspirational. Convictions describe who we are, not who we want to become.

They are truly and passionately held. This belief system is not something that is learned or created. It is not what you hope to become. It is who you are – your core.

You should address your Core Convictions as they truly exist, not as you want them to be.

If you don't, those around you will not be able to believe in you or your vision.

We hold our Core Convictions even if they become a competitive disadvantage. We would not change our convictions in response to market changes – we would rather change markets to remain true to Core Convictions.

Your convictions improve clarity and decision-making because all decisions are filtered through them.

So, ask the following questions to determine your Core Convictions.

1. What do I stand for? Why do I exist? What convictions do I personally bring to work?

2. How would I describe my Core Convictions to my children?
3. If I were to start a new organization tomorrow in a different line of work, what Core Convictions would I bring to it?

Once you write your list of convictions, evaluate them by asking:

If I had enough money to retire, would I continue to live these Core Convictions?

Do I envision them being just as valid 20 years from now as they are today?

Would I hold these Core Convictions even if one or more of them became a competitive disadvantage in the marketplace?

I have four Core Convictions that serve as a filter for all of my decisions.

Here they are:

1. Everything I do connects people with God more substantively.

2. I am committed to the ongoing development of talented team members, and I am strategic about who is added to my team and how I develop their unlimited potential.

3. I maintain simplicity in processes and procedures to focus on delivering WOW experiences through great service.

4. I am committed to great decisions based on solid research and data.

Now, list your Core Convictions

With relentless honesty, identify 3-5 Core Convictions that are truly central to your life and work. Remember, convictions must stand the test of time.

1. _____
   _____

2. _____
   _____

3. _____
   _____

4. _____
   _____

5. _____
   _____

Core Purpose

Your Core Purpose is what you are all about. It is your reason for existing and reflects your deepest motivation for doing your work. It captures your soul and the soul of your team or organization.

It reveals who you exist to serve and why, and includes how you will impact the marketplace.

Your Core Purpose should elicit emotion within your team and your market.

In the Harvard Business Review article, Building Your Company's Vision, Collins and Porras observed that you can fulfill your purpose every single day, but you will never achieve your purpose. It's something that you constantly pursue throughout your life.

So, ask these questions to determine your Core Purpose.

1. Why are your products or services important? Once you have that answer, then ask, Why is THAT important? Then ask it again. And again - five times. After a few "whys" you'll find that you are getting down to the core of your fundamental purpose.

2. Suppose you went out of business and your products or services were discontinued. Your operations shut down. The organization ceased to exist. What would be lost? Why is it important that it continues to exist?

3. If you had enough money to retire, would you still keep doing what you do? If so, why?

For example, here's my Core Purpose

To enable purposeful and lasting life-change within every person I lead and coach so they achieve maximum growth and health in their life and work.

Now, write your Core Purpose

_____

_____

CORE PURPOSE

_____

_____

_____

_____

Envisioned Future

Now that you've defined your Core Purpose, you can focus on what lies ahead. Your Envisioned Future involves what you will build and what you will become. When the future is clear, you can form plans to make it happen.

So, what are you building and who are you becoming as a result of showing up every day?

The Envisioned Future consists of two parts:

1. **Huge Goals.** What are you building?

2. **Vivid Description.** What it will be like to achieve the goal. What are you becoming?

Here's how the team at Building Champions describes Envisioned Future:

CREATING YOUR BUSINESS VISION

" We're inviting people on a journey — taking them to the base of Mount Everest, pointing to the summit, and inviting them to go with us. For others to decide if they want to make the trek, they need to know what the journey is going to look like.

Why is it important that they understand the journey? Because somewhere between Kathmandu and the summit of Mount Everest a storm is going to hit, supplies will run low, there will be disagreements, tempers are going to flare, there will be challenges, there will be struggles."

Are you currently experiencing a challenging situation at work?

The Envisioned Future allows you and the team to come back to it — to see that you expected the struggles and challenges. It reminds you where you are headed — who you are becoming.

The Envisioned Future is the mountain to be climbed. It needs to be so compelling that it keeps your organization motivated long into the future, even after you retire or move on.

Huge Goals

There is a fundamental difference between merely having a goal and committing to a huge, exhilarating challenge. Jim Collins, best-selling author of Great by Choice, calls these huge goals Big, Hairy, Audacious Goals or BHAGS.

Daniel Harkavy refers to them as Mount Everest Goals. They are clear and compelling. They serve as unifying focal points of effort and act as catalysts for team spirit. They have a clear finish line – your team will know when it has achieved the goal. They are tangible, energizing, and highly focused.

So, ask these questions to determine your Mount Everest Goals.

1. What are we building?
2. Where do we want to go?
3. What will we be the best at?

CREATING YOUR BUSINESS VISION

After you draft your goals, evaluate them by asking:

1. Is it specific? Is it clear?

2. Is it measurable?

3. Is it time-sensitive? When will you achieve it?

4. Will it stretch you? If you are leading a team, your Mount Everest Goals should be appropriate for you and your team and should inspire them.

5. Does it inspire a long-term commitment to the adventure? Goals that require only short-term commitments are not Mount Everest Goals.

6. Will some doubt your (or your team's) ability to accomplish it? People should question how you will accomplish your Mount Everest Goals.

My wife, Sarah, recently developed a vision for her counseling work. Here are a few examples of her Mount Everest Goals:

1. Partner with a counseling organization, large corporation, or university with strong Christian convictions and high interest in innovative coaching and counseling development.

HUGE GOALS

2. Develop a 50 to 100 acre nationally-known retreat center equipped with 15-20 spacious, self-sufficient rooms in which clients are able to focus, relax, heal, and re-energize.

3. Counsel 250 clients annually.

4. Coach 50 clients annually.

5. Become the model process and center for coaching and counseling.

You may have noticed – these are huge goals!

Your Mount Everest Goals should attract some cynics and naysayers. In fact, even I question how Sarah will accomplish some of these. But I've already seen the remarkable progress she's made toward them in a short period of time.

Your goals should be huge! If your goals aren't ambitious and challenging, they're probably not worth attempting. So, in a way, your critics are right – you can't get there; not on your own. But together with your team, with your partners, with your customers – you can get there.

Now you're ready to write your Mount Everest Goals

1. _____

_____

CREATING YOUR BUSINESS VISION

2. _____

_____

3. _____

_____

4. _____

_____

5. _____

_____

Now, circle the ONE goal that represents your Mount Everest summit. What does the top of the mountain look like for you and your team?

Vivid Description

The Vivid Description is a specific, vibrant, and engaging description of what it will be like to achieve your Mount Everest Goals. It translates the vision and goals from words into pictures. A compelling Vivid Description includes passion, emotion, and conviction.

Ask yourself the following questions to create your Vivid Description

1. What will the organization (or department or position) become in the future?

2. What will it look like for team members?

3. How will it make clients more successful?

4. We're sitting here in 10, 20, 30 years – what would we love to see?

5. What should the organization (or department or position) look like?

6. What should it feel like to my team?

7. What should it have achieved?

8. If someone writes an article for a major business magazine about the organization (or department or position) in 10 years, what will it say?

As you draft the Vivid Description, consider the key areas of your organization, products, and services.

Some of them may be:

- **Leadership**
- **Training**
- **Marketing**
- **Sales**
- **Communication**
- **Celebrations**

For example - Leadership. What does the leadership team look like that is able to reach 29,035 feet, the summit of Mount Everest? If you don't already have these people on your team, you will need to develop them or you will need to find new team members.

Here is an example of a Vivid Description

This is an excerpt from Sarah's Vivid Description for a coaching and counseling retreat center:

> The retreat center surpasses every person's imagination – it is an oasis that is professional yet personal.
>
> The retreat grounds are immaculate and peaceful in every season. The furniture and décor is current and welcoming. A housekeeping team gives attention to every detail throughout the center. An executive chef prepares the finest cuisine.
>
> Teams, couples, and individuals discover a relaxing place to stay providing relief and rest from pressures of life and work. Guests enjoy spa services free of charge through donor scholarships.
>
> Therapeutic art experiences allow clients to process thoughts, feelings, and behaviors and obtain clarity. Walking trails that lead through wooded forests and serene outdoor recreation facilitate reflection and focus. The center is safe, secure, and serene.
>
> The retreat center is a place for non-clients to visit, stay, utilize the prayer garden, relax in

CREATING YOUR BUSINESS VISION

the spa environment which includes an indoor pool, spa, and fitness center, or simply get away for a few days.

The center will include office space, a library, an industrial kitchen, and innovative meeting and educational space to accommodate up to 75 people.

Now, write your Vivid Description

You will likely need a page or two for your Vivid Description.

_____

_____

_____

_____

_____

_____

_____

_____

_____

VIVID DESCRIPTION

Get It All Together

Now take everything you have documented above and compile your vision document.

List the components in the following order: Core Convictions, Core Purpose, Mount Everest Goals, and Vivid Description.

Then, most importantly, **share your vision every chance you get!** Talk about it daily in your interactions with colleagues. Illustrate it and share success stories in your regular team meetings. Use it when hiring new team members. They should have the opportunity to decide if they are interested in going on the journey with you – before they accept the position.

Use it in employee evaluations as you assess performance and communicate new objectives. Use it when developing and updating business plans and strategic initiatives.

Use it. Use it. Use it.

Your work, your team, your influence, your leadership, your energy, will never be the same. Because of this one purposeful decision.

When you can see it – you can build it!

If you have just been reading through, you're now ready to develop your vision step by step.

To get you started, I have included space throughout the book for developing your vision.

It's possible to succeed in your work without a Business Vision, just as you can find your way to a destination without a map. But it is easier with a written vision, and you and others are more likely to enjoy the journey.

So, plan right now when you are going to write your Business Vision.

Review and Communicate It

Your vision must be regularly reviewed and communicated, or it will have little impact on your life and work.

So, once you complete it, the first thing to do is establish a weekly time to review it. I go over my Business Vision every Monday morning during my weekly review.

Then, communicate it every chance you get – to your team, within your organization, with potential employees, with new vendors and customers.

To accomplish vision, a change in culture must occur. And, when it is regularly and clearly communicated, people have the opportunity to understand, take ownership, and live out the vision. So talk about it everywhere you go.

A Growing Leader

I am a visionary person – vision comes natural to me. For much of my career, vision resided primarily in my head and in my heart – but not in writing. As a result, I was unable to gain the traction in areas of my work that were high priority areas for me. And my teams and organizations didn't reach our fullest potential.

While my vision was crystal clear to me, it was not specific and compelling for my colleagues because it was not written and communicated effectively. It had not become tangible to them.

So I did something about it – I wrote out my vision.

Writing out my vision brought clarity and focus to my work.

Vision – written vision – became the subconscious filter for my career and work decisions. It simplified countless decisions. In many cases, the vision increased the speed and implementation of new initiatives.

Nailing this one discipline – the Business Vision – has given me the focus and energy I needed to intentionally improve other areas of my life and work that are important to me. My written vision has opened the door for me to share my progress – my story – with others and to encourage them to grow on purpose.

My life plan and business vision include specific commitments and huge goals – for my health, my family, my team, my institution. And **pursuing these goals with purpose has paid off.**

One of my colleagues noticed recently that I had lost significant weight. I wasn't trying to lose weight – although I needed to! I simply began eating more healthy and working out more regularly. You can read the full article on my blog - Why I Changed My Diet and How I Lost 30 Pounds.

Since my vision is clearly defined, I am communicating it with more clarity and consistency.

And I have seen dramatic relational improvements in teams and organizations as I have worked with them to develop and communicate vision. After a series of recent meetings, several individuals emailed me to let me know that they had noticed significant progress in my interactions with my teams and colleagues.

Another team member recently commented to me about our team – **They really love you.**

I hate to admit it, but it's the first time I've ever been told that by a team member. In fact, it was several team members who encouraged me to expand this conclusion to include how my vision has profoundly impacted my life – so I did.

So, get ready for extraordinary results – your work will never be the same!

Your Voice Matters

I'd love to hear your thoughts – what you liked, what didn't make sense, what impacted you, etc. Share your feedback by...

1. Leaving a review on Amazon and Barnes and Noble. If you don't do anything else, do this! There are a lot of books out there. And the ones that spread do so because people keep talking about them. When you tell a friend about Creating Your Business Vision or leave a review, it does more than you will ever know.
2. Commenting on my blog post. www.miken.co/CommentCBV
3. Emailing me. michael@michaelnichols.org

What you think, matters to me. It helps me to continue to improve content and resources for you and many others like you.

Thank you so much for your continued support of my new book! It means the world to me. Now, let me know how I can serve you. Seriously!

Resources

Here are a few of the resources I have found most helpful in creating a Business Vision and living an intentional life.

Jim Collins and Jerry Porras, *Building Your Company's Vision*, Harvard Business Review (September, 1996)

Stephen Covey, *The 7 Habits of Highly Effective People: Powerful Lessons in Personal Change* (New York: Free Press, Revised Edition, 2004)

Michael Gerber, *The E-Myth Revisited: Why Most Small Businesses Don't Work and What to Do About It* (New York: HarperCollins, 1995)

Daniel Harkavy, *Becoming a Coaching Leader: The Proven Strategy for Building Your Own Team of Champions* (Nashville: Thomas Nelson, 2007)

Michael Hyatt, *Creating Your Personal Life Plan*, (2011)

RESOURCES

Ken Blanchard and Mark Miller, *Great Leaders Grow*, (San Francisco: Berrett-Koehler, 2012)

Jim Collins, *Great by Choice*, (New York: Harper Collins, 2011)

Jon Acuff, *Start: Punch Fear in the Face, Escape Average*, (Nashville: Thomas Nelson, 2013)

Building Champions

If you really want to take your life and business planning to the next level, consider an executive coach from Building Champions. Many of the concepts included in this book I have learned from the Building Champions team. I have greatly benefited from my experience with Building Champions and highly recommend them.

www.buildingchampions.com

Contact

After you read this book, I'd love to hear about your experience writing your Business Vision. Contact me using one of the links below:

Blog   http://michaelnichols.org

Facebook http://fb.com/nicholsm

Twitter   http://twitter.com/michaelenichols

LinkedIn http://linkedin.com/in/nicholsmichael

Email   michael@michaelnichols.org

Share It With Others!

If you found this book helpful, please share it with others. We've made it easy for you - use the links below!

Post a comment - miken.co/CommentCBV

Share on Twitter - miken.co/TweetCBV

Share on Facebook - miken.co/FacebookCBV